1 MONTH OF
FREE
READING

at

www.ForgottenBooks.com

By purchasing this book you are eligible for one month membership to ForgottenBooks.com, giving you unlimited access to our entire collection of over 1,000,000 titles via our web site and mobile apps.

To claim your free month visit:

www.forgottenbooks.com/free835971

ISBN 978-0-666-33077-2
PIBN 10835971

QUEEN VICTORIA

AND HER REIGN.

A Biography, with references to the Literature, Art,
Commerce, and National Development of
the last fifty years.

————— ·◄●►· —————

HERE has probably never been a period in the history of the world when such vast
and beneficent changes have taken place in all matters relating to the welfare of
mankind, as in the reign of Victoria, Queen of Great Britain and Ireland, and
Empress of India. These changes have not, indeed, resembled the sudden convul-
sions of nature, which uproot forests, overthrow mountains, turn the course of rivers,
and devastate the world; but are rather to be compared to the effect of the gentle summer rain,
which distils through the soil till it reaches the very roots of vegetation, and clothes the
earth with a mantle of beauty. · For it is a happy peculiarity of the material and social im-
provement characterising the nineteenth century, that it reaches to the lowest condition of
life; and the masses of the people have perhaps derived more solid advantages from it than
have any other classes of society. It is true that the surroundings of existence are now so
different from what they were at the commencement of Her Majesty's reign, that if *any* man
who died half a century ago could revisit the earth, he would find himself practically in a new
world, bewildered by the presence of a variety of things which to him would be devoid of
meaning; but the difference produced by the resources of modern civilization is even more
perceptible in the lower than in the higher ranks. By the marvellous facility and consequent
cheapness of production, with the ever-increasing multitude of products, the artisan of the
present day finds himself in posession of comforts and even luxuries which princes of past
generations had no conception of. The whole course of modern legislation, too, has a similar
tendency. Laws are no longer made for the benefit of a few, but for the general well-being of
the people. Men high in social rank, possessors of noble names and exalted positions, have
made it the business and the joy of their lives to alleviate the distreseses of those around them,
and to elevate them in the scale of humanity. How much of this may be owing to the
gracious example of the present occupant of the throne, and of her noble and devoted husband,
the late lamented Prince Consort, Albert the Good, it is difficult to estimate; certain it is that
Her Majesty has ever shown the warmest interest in all that concerns the happiness of her
subjects, and that much of the attachment felt for her personally, and for the Royalty of which
she is the representative, undoubtedly proceeds from her sympathy with suffering, her
appreciation of excellence, and the manner in which she identifies herself with those over whom
she rules. These are qualities which can be understood and admired by millions on whom
dignified deportment, mental accomplishment, and skill in state-craft could make no impres-
sion; and they do more than armed battalions to support the throne from which they
emanate.

Issued by W. F. BURNSIDE; Printed by the "Herald" Company, Montreal.

KENSINGTON PALACE,

Sixty-eight years ago, a baby was born at Kensington Palace, about whom the world thought very little at the time, although she brought great joy to the hearts of her loving father and mother. Her father was the Duke of Kent, fourth son of the reigning King, George III.

Of course the royal family took some interest in the arrival of the little stranger, and her grandfather, the King, wanted her to be named Georgiana. Her father wished her to be called Elizabeth, because it was a favorite name among English people, but her uncle, the Prince Regent, insisted that she should be called Alexandrina after the Emperor of Russia. Victoria was added as an afterthought, but little Drina was her name through all her early years.

She was not at her birth the recognized heiress of the crown. As we have said, her father, Edward, Duke of Kent, was the fourth (and the best) son of George the Third. George the Fourth, the eldest son and successor of that monarch, left but one child, the Princess Charlotte, who died about a year and a half after her marriage, her baby-boy dying with her. The Duke of York, second son of George the Third, died unmarried, without coming to the throne. The Duke of Clarence, his brother, reigned as William the Fourth, after the death of the Fourth George; he had two little daughters, but both died in infancy. It was not till these successive events had taken place, that it began to be clear that the daughter of the Duke of Kent would be the future Queen of England. Her father died in the year 1820, when she was only eight months old, leaving her to the charge of her widowed mother, by whom she was trained with a careful wisdom which has been the theme of universal admiration To that good and self-sacrificing woman England owes much, for she devoted herself to the cultivation of her daughter's mind; inculcating not only the principles of religion and virtue by which the life of the Queen has been regulated, but all those "minor moralities" of method, exactness, punctuality, and faithfulness to engagements which have been of incalculable service

THE QUEEN AT THIRTEEN.

in public business. The childhood of Victoria seems never to have been idle : "all her moments were golden—for study, or work, or healthful exercise, or play." She is described by Lord Albemarle as being (at seven years old) a "bright, pretty little girl;" by Lord Campbell as "lively and good humoured." Other observers give instances of her thoughtful kindness; and every bud of promise was tenderly cultured by her judicious mother.

A tourist of more than half a century ago tells us how he wandered one day into the churchyard of Brading, in the Isle of Wight, to see the grave of Elizabeth Wallbridge, whose early piety is recorded in Leigh Richmond's beautiful story of " The Dairyman's Daughter." He found seated beside the mound a lady and a young girl ; the young girl reading aloud, in a full melodious voice, the touching tale of the Christian maiden. The tourist turned away

THE CORONATION

and was told by the sexton that these pilgrims to that humble grave were the Duchess of Kent
and the Princess Victoria.

The influence of such a mother was doubtless to be seen in Queen Victoria's admirable
training of her own little ones, and her simple, domestic, affectionate system of home management. The instructions given by Her Majesty to the Governess of the Princess Royal might
be printed in letters of gold :—" She should be taught to have great reverence for God and
for religion, and the feeling of devotion and love which our Heavenly father encourages His
earthly children to have for Him."

It was not till the Princess Victoria was about 12 years of age that she was allowed to
know her true position, and her nearness to the crown. She received the information thought-

E. & C. GURNEY & CO.,

385 & 387 ST. PAUL ST., MONTREAL,

WHOLESALE MANUFACTURERS

Stoves, Grates, Ranges, Scales.

GURNEY'S CELEBRATED HOT WATER HEATERS,

—— AND ——

CAST BUNDY RADIATORS.

HOT AIR FURNACES FOR COAL OR WOOD.

All Goods Guaranteed.   Circulars on Application.

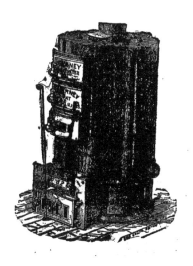

THE QUEEN IN 1840.

sally, with the remark "There is much splendour, but there is also much responsibility." She said to the Baròness Lehzen, her governess, "I will be good. I understand now why you have urged me so much to learn;" and the Baroness adds "The princess gave me her hand, repeating, 'I will be good.' Surely there was promise of the greatness and glory of her reign in such a reception of the news of her dazzling destiny!

In the year 1837 King William the Fourth passed away. The King had greatly desired to live until his niece came of age—which would be at the age of eighteen—so that she herself might ascend the throne without the need of a regency under the Duchess of Kent; and the wish was gratified. Princess Drina came of age May 24th, 1837, and William IV. lived until the 19th of the following month.

Although his death had been almost hourly expected for some days previously, the little household at Kensington Palace went on as usual until it was aroused by a loud knocking at the outer gate in the summer dawn of June 20th, when the porter hastily summoned some of the servants and told them that the Archbishop of Canterbury and the Home Secretary had come to see the Princess.

"But she is asleep, and it is only five o'clock in the morning," said the surprised servant.

"No matter what the time is. I must see the Princess at once," said the Archbishop; and so the servant went to summon her.

The lady did not keep him waiting so long as her servants had done. In her white night-dress, with a shawl drawn round her shoulders and her long, fair hair falling down her back, she hastened to the parlor where the Archbishop was waiting, and there received the

PRINCE ALBERT AT THE TIME OF HIS MARRIAGE.

news that she was now Queen of England. For a minute she stood silent and awestruck after he had done speaking, and then said, "I ask your prayers on my behalf." It was a reign fitly begun—in simple dependence upon God—and amply has He blessed her who thus cast herself upon His care.

Until after her accession it was not known that we should have a Queen Victoria. All the documents had been prepared in the name she had hitherto been known by—Alexandrina —but after her first Council meeting, when called upon to sign her name for the first time as sovereign, she wrote 'Victoria.'

The Coronation took place in Westminster Abbey on June 28th, 1838. It was a wonderful and impressive scene, and the young Queen went bravely through her part in the long series of ceremonies connected with the service.

Possibly many supposed that a young girl only eighteen would be willing to do exactly as she was told by her Council and the Prime Minister, but Lord Melbourne soon discovered that she had a will of her own. When a document was brought to her to sign she not only insisted upon reading it through, but asked questions about its details, and sometimes declined to affix her signature until she had further time for consideration. "It is with me a matter of paramount importance whether or not I attach my signature to a document with which I am thoroughly satsified," she said one day when her Minister was urging her to sign her name at

BEAVER LINE.

PASSENGER STEAMSHIPS
REGULAR SERVICE BETWEEN

MONTREAL & LIVERPOOL

PASSENGERS BOOKED TO AND FROM ALL PARTS OF EUROPE.

STEAMERS ARE ALL OF THE HIGHEST CLASS.

AND HAVE SUPERIOR ACCOMMODATION FOR

SALOON,
SECOND CABIN AND
STEERAGE PASSENGERS

RATES OF PASSAGE AS LOW AS BY ANY OTHER FIRST CLASS LINE

OUTWARD AND PRE-PAID STEERAGE TICKETS AT LOWEST RATES

ALL PASSENGERS EMBARK AND LAND AT MONTREAL.

A liberal allowance of Baggage Free.

Qualified Surgeons and Experienced Stewardesses accompany these Steamers.

The Company Endeavours to make each Passenger an advertisement for the Line.

For freight or other particulars, apply : In Belfast, to A. A. WATT, 8 Custom House Square; in Queenstown, to N. G. SEYMOUR & Co. ; in Liverpool, to R. W. ROBERTS, 21 Water Street; in Quebec, to H. H. SEWELL, 125 Peter Street.

H. E. MURRAY, General Manager,
1 Custom House Square, MONTREAL.

WINDSOR CASTLE.

D. McCall & Co.

OF TORONTO,

WHOLESALE

Millinery, Mantles ————o

———AND———

o———— Fancy Dry Goods.

MONTREAL BRANCH
"GLENORA BUILDINGS,"
1888 NOTRE DAME STREET,
MONTREAL.

WILLIAM J. O'MALLEY,
Agent.

THE PRINCE OF WALES.

-once. Another time he submitted an Act for her signature and urged expediency, when she stopped him, exclaiming, "I have been taught, my lord, to judge what is right and wrong, but expediency is a word which I neither wish to hear nor understand." No wonder Lord Melbourne exclaimed after this that he would rather have ten kings to manage than one queen, for such uncompromising behaviour in political matters was a thing almost unknown.

The entrance upon such responsible duties by one so young and inexperienced must indeed have caused grave anxiety both to herself and her friends. Public feeling was at that time a good deal excited from various causes, and a vast amount of passion and ignorance was manifested, making the work of Constitutional Government difficult. But, amidst all

BALMORAL.

difficulties, the Divine protection, so needed, and so earnestly besought, has not been withheld; and the reign of Victoria has not only been long, but prosperous.

Never has England had so constitutional a Sovereign, or one giving more attention to all the duties of Government, and thus we have a throne firmly seated in the love and loyalty of the people, while other thrones have been tottering, and some have been overturned.

As Queen and Mother—in public and private life—in the cares of government and the management of a household, Victoria had the inestimable advantage resulting from union with a pure and noble character like that of her beloved husband, Prince Albert. In philosophy and science, in music and in practical life, he was equally at home ; his excellent disposition and admirable training alike fitted him for the difficult and important part he had to play. The letter he wrote to his grandmother, the Dowager Duchess of Saxe-Cobourg, on his wedding day, is sufficient to show his earnest, thoughtful spirit :—

"Dear Grandmama ; in less than three hours I shall stand at the altar with my dear bride. In these solemn moments I must once more ask your blessing, which I am well assured I shall receive, and which will be my safeguard and future joy. I must end. God be my stay !

"Your faithful

"ALBERT."

The marriage was exceptionally fortunate in being one of affection. Queens and princes have often to study the likings and dislikings of others rather than their own, and defer to reasons of state and the convenience of their subjects. But to this couple was granted a domestic happiness rare even among the obscure. Prince Albert, from the very first, seems

PRINCESS LOUISE.   MARQUIS OF LORNE.

to have resolved to put aside every personal predilection in order to pursue that course which should be best for his wife (as the Queen loved to call herself) and his adopted country. No wonder that he secured for himself a high place in the affection of the monarch and the esteem of her subjects. At first, it is true, there were strong prejudices against him, and misrepresentation of his character and motives, curious to look back upon in the light of succeeding events ; but these could not withstand the influence of his unswerving fidelity to principle and lofty disinterestedness. When his untimely death took place, at the age of 42, it was found that he was regarded with a loving veneration only second to that paid to the Sovereign herself.

That he possessed great energy and perseverance is evidenced by the Great Exhibition of 1851, the idea of which was first conceived by him, as by his influence and active exertion it was carried into practical execution. It seems surprising now to reflect on the opposition it encountered. Colonel Sibthorp declared in the House of Commons that the enemy of mankind had inspired the idea, so that foreigners might rob us of our trade and our honour, and complete the ruin of the nation which Free Trade had commenced. The House of Lords was petitioned to refuse Hyde Park as a site ; Lord Brougham attacked the scheme with vehemence ; and there was in many quarters a dread lest the assembling of such a vast concourse of people might lead to scenes of danger and violence. Unquestionably, but for the force of character of the Prince Consort the matter would have been abandoned. But the result justified his conception and his efforts. "The great event," wrote the Queen after the opening, "has taken place—a complete and beautiful triumph—a glorious and touching sight, one which I shall ever be proud of for my beloved Albert and my country. Such efforts have been made, and our people have shown such taste in their manufactures. All owing to this great Exhibition, and to Albert ; all to *him*." We cannot wonder that she who wrote thus felt a deep and lasting sorrow at the loss of this great and good man, or that she cherishes a tender regard for his memory.

The allusion to the Great Exhibition of 1851 reminds us of the wonderful advances which have been made during the present reign, not only in arts and manufactures, but in all matters affecting the public good. According to a high authority, the average earnings of the working classes in this country have been doubled during the last 50 years, while in the same period the purchasing power of money has not materially depreciated. What home comforts could possibly have been enjoyed in a labourer's cottage when 8s. per week was not an unusual pay ?—when we read of a half-fed, poorly-clad family of eight or nine, including two grown up young men, and two young women, habitually sleeping in one room, as many as

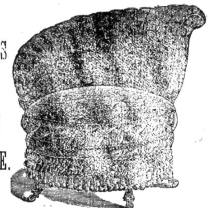

THE QUEEN IN 1861.

possible in one bed? Then, too, the Corn-Laws kept up the price of food, and brought the poor to the verge of starvation; being (as Lord John Russell expressed it) "the cause of penury, fever, mortality, and crime." But by the terrible famine in Ireland in 1845 (caused by the failure of the potato crop) the hands of Free-traders were so much strengthened that Sir Robert Peel was enabled to carry the abolition of the Corn Laws in 1846; and now as he himself said, "men whose lot it is to labour can recruit their exhausted strength with abundant and untaxed food, the sweeter because it is no longer leavened with a sense of injustice."

When the Earl of Shaftesbury (then Lord Ashley) commenced his efforts for procuring the Acts of Parliament regulating the employment of women and children in mines and factories,

THE NEW WILLIAMS MACHINE

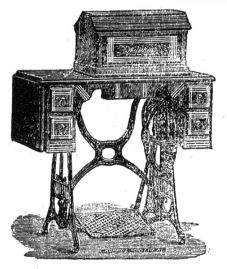

Is made of the best material, and finished with the greatest care, and in the most perfect manner. It runs very light and easy, the motion being smooth and free from jar or vibration. It is as nearly noiseless as it is possible for a shuttle Sewing machine to be made.

The arm is high, large and roomy, affording ample space through which to pass the work and manipulate heavy garments, etc.

All kinds of work can be done on the NEW WILLIAMS, from an ordinary plain seam to the most beautiful and intricate patterns in embroidery. The finest cambric or muslin can be sewn with the same facility as the heavier grades of work. a strong, elastic and perfect stitch being made on all kinds of material.

—o—

Factories at MONTREAL, Canada, and PLATTSBURG, New York State.

HEAD OFFICE FOR THE DOMINION :

1733 Notre Dame St.,
MONTREAL.

CHARLES GURD & CO.,
BELFAST × GINGER × ALE
—AND—
SODA   WATER   MANUFACTURERS.

GOLD, SILVER AND BRONZE MEDALS AWARDED
FOR SUPERIOR EXCELLENCE.

Ask Your Grocer for GURD'S GINGER ALE, SODA WATER and CHAMPAGNE CIDER.

WHOLESALE ONLY FROM THE FACTORY :

39 to 49 JURORS ST.
MONTREAL.

THE QUEEN IN 1884.

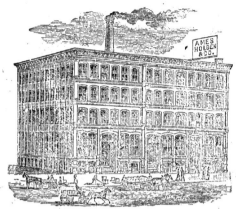

AMES, HOLDEN & CO,

ESTABLISHED 1853.

MANUFACTURERS AND WHOLESALE DEALERS
—IN—

BOOTS AND SHOES

Rubbers,

Moccassins,

Beef Boots,

Blacking,

Dressings, Laces, etc., etc.

Having one of the largest and best equipped Factories in Canada, with all the latest and most improved machinery, we are in a position to supply the Trade with first-class goods at moderate prices.

FINE GOODS A SPECIALTY.

❋BRANCH HOUSES❋

Winnepeg, Man., AND
Victoria, B.C.

LORD LANDSDOWNE.

it was shown that in some of the coal mines women were employed literally as beasts of burden. Where the seam of coal was too narrow for them to stand upright, they had to crawl backward and forward on all fours from 14 to 16 hours a day, dragging trucks laden with coal. Their only clothing often consisted of an old pair of trousers made of sacking. All manner of hideous diseases were generated in these unsexed bodies. Kindred horrors existed in other departments of labour, but were put an end to by the acts of 1842 and 1844.

Such a change must have been peculiarly acceptable to the Sovereign, who has ever been foremost in the relief of distress, and who has shown so profound and practical a sympathy with the poor and the sick, the helpless and the unfortunate.

Our Royal Family have always shown a deep interest in all that might tend to elevate

SIR DONALD A. SMITH.

the people. The late Prince Consort possessed a many sided mind, and in every direction his influence for good was felt, particularly in fostering the spread of education, and the promotion of art and science. Sir James Kaye Shuttleworth informs us that Her Majesty shows her own feeling in the matter by founding and sustaining schools near Windsor at a cost of £1,000 a year, to say nothing of innumerable acts of munificence in other directions.

In practical science, the advances made during the present reign have been truly marvellous, and such as could not have entered into the wildest imagination of our forefathers. The railway system alone has fairly revolutionized society. Though it was inaugurated before Queen Victoria came to the throne, it has received its mighty development under her Government. Even the London and Birmingham line was not opened throughout its whole length till 1838, and a writer of the period speaks of "the prospect of travelling from the metropolis to Liverpool (a distance of 210 miles) in ten hours, "as calling to mind the ta'es of fairies and genii by which we were amused in our youth." How can we estimate the effect of this potent engine of Civilization, the Railway System, in bringing together separated communities, curing ignorance, and removing prejudice?

It was also in the first year of Her Majesty's reign that the problem of ocean steamboat navigation was practically solved by the successful voyage of the "Great Western" and other vessels, notwithstanding the declaration of a noble lord that he would engage "to eat the boiler of the first steamboat that crossed the Atlantic." But as subject of wonder, these achievements are overshadowed by the Electric Telegraph, which has more than fulfilled the fanciful boast of Shakespeare's "dainty Ariel," that he would "put a girdle round the earth

The Royal Electric Co'y.

OFFICE, FACTORY AND LIGHTING STATION,

Nos. 54, 56, 58 & 60 Wellington St.,

MONTREAL.

Proprietors of the Thompson, Houston system of Electric Lighting for the Dominion of Canada.

Manufacturers of Electric Dynamos, Lamps, and all materials used in the business of Electric Lighting.

CONTRACTORS FOR THE ERECTION OF ELECTRIC PLANTS THROUGHOUT THE DOMINION. TENDERS AND ALL INFORMATION GIVEN ON APPLICATION.

CHARLES W. HAGAR,
MANAGER.

The MONTREAL BISCUIT Co

JAS. W. TESTER, *President.* JAS. McBRIDE, *Vice President.*

JOHN FARQUARSON, *Managing Director.*

MANUFACTURERS OF ALL KINDS OF

BISCUITS AND CRACKERS,

82 AND 84 McGILL STREET,
AND
95 AND 97 GREY NUN STREET,

MONTREAL.

!SIR GEORGE STEPHEN.

in forty minutes." The Telephone, a recent development of the same principle, enables us to speak to a person miles away, and receive his reply with as much ease, and almost as much speed, as if he were in the same room with us. Still more astounding are the Microphone and Phonograph: in the latter instrument we may bottle up the voice of a friend and reproduce it at any time for our enjoyment. The applications of electricity, indeed, appear limitless; already carriages are driven by it; buildings and streets are lighted by it; and it seems destined to be the "force of the future."

Since the remote period when the wisdom and forethought of the patriotic King Alfred laid the foundation of a navy, England has been indebted to her sailors not only for defence, but for much of her material prosperity.

Of late years great changes have taken place in the construction of the navy, royal and mercantile: steam and iron have supplemented the powers of canvas and wood, and are aiding Britannia to "rule the waves." The expansion of commerce in the last half century is

E. A. SMALL & CO'Y.,

Montreal.

Manufacturers of

CLOTHING

WHOLESALE.

marvellous. The navigation laws, once supposed to be essential to the protection of the British shipping interests, were repealed as far back as the time of George the Fourth. Various restrictions, however, were retained till the present reign, but are now abandoned. Of course it was prognosticated that if this step were taken, and if foreigners were allowed equal privileges with Englishmen in trade and shipping, the result would be most disastrous : but, as is so often the case, facts have falsified the predictions. British enterprise awoke, and it is not too much to say that the great bulk of the commerce of the world is now carried on in British ships, which are to be found studding the bosom of the ocean, and lying in every harbour. The present Royal family, as becomes their English birth, are sea lovers. The Queen is a frequent voyager : her son, the Duke of Edinburgh, holds an important command in the Navy : two of her grandsons, children of the Prince of Wales, are in training for the same noble profession : so that full emphasis is given to the sense entertained of the importance of the Navy to England's greatness.

It is doubtless owing, in some measure, to England's command of the sea that she is great in Colonies. Of course there are other important reasons. The Anglo-Saxon-Celtic-Danish-Norman race (known as English) has always shown an instinct for colonization, and the pressure of population demands an outlet. At all events, notwithstanding the loss of our American Colonies in the reign of George the Third, those now connected with England are superior in extent and resources to some independent nations, and are destined to play an important part in the world's history. Immense accessions have been made to their power and population during the present reign. Take this Canada of ours for example. Descriptions of Canada are as plentiful as blackberries in Autumn, but we do not propose to enter into one of these descriptions. Suffice it to say that Canada offers a home where all the conveniences of life may be enjoyed at far less cost than can be obtained in old England, and this too at a period when the circumstances of thousands are comparatively straitened at home.

Her British constitution ensures perfect security to life and property. Her railways and her lakes and rivers ; and the shortness of the voyage across, enable her to invite all to come and try her climate ; her facilities for retrenchment, without curtailing in any degree the enjoyment of all the necessarses of life, or abandoning anything except positive luxuries. Other colonies may offer greater inducements to those in search of a speedy fortune (although this may be called in question). The adventures of bush life may be far more exciting at the Cape, its difficulties and trials incomparably less, and a profitable return for exertion may perhaps be secured elsewhere in less time ; but no colony equally accessible offers the same advantages to those who have no desire to rough it in the bush, on the one hand, nor yet to join in the gaieties and expenses of town life, on the other, but simply to keep the middle course ; they can do this by securing any of the innumerable farms within a mile or two of the railways, which now run throughout the entire length and breadth of Canada.

The progress of this Dominion, has indeed been wonderful. In many places, where but a comparatively short time ago small towns existed, we have now large and prosperous cities. And here a few words about the city of Montreal may not be out of place.

Montreal, the largest city in Canada, and the chief seat of commerce and principal port of entry, is situated on an island of about 30 miles in length, and 7 in breadth, at the confluence of the rivers Ottawa & St. Lawrence. It stands at the head of ocean navigation, 160 miles above Quebec, and nearly 1000 miles from the Atlantic Ocean, and lies at the foot of the great chain of river, lake, and canal navigation which extends westward through the great lakes. Montreal is built upon a series of terraces, the former levels of the river, or of a more ancient sea. Behind those rises Mount Royal, from which the city derives its name. From its commanding site, and the wide expanse of the valley of the St. Lawrence, the views on all sides are of great variety and beauty. Two islands, the Nun's and St. Helen's Isles – the latter beautifully wooded, and laid out as a public park—occupy the bed of the river immediately below the Lachine Rapids, and between them the river is spanned by the great Victoria Bridge. This wonderful triumph of engineering skill is a tubular iron bridge supported on twenty-four piers of solid masonry, with the terminal abutments of the same, and measuring 9184 feet in length. The river descends at the rate of seven miles an hour at the point where it is crossed ; and the piers are constructed with a view to resist the enormous pressure of the ice in spring. The wharves and docks are crowded with shipping during the season of navigation, for the St. Lawrence is navigable to Montreal by the largest ocean steamers. The fall of water in the canal furnishes water power for saw mills, boiler and engine works, sash, blind, door, edge tools, and other factories established on its banks. Sugar refining has also been carried on here with great profit. Woolen and cotton mills, silk factories, a large rubber factory, rope and cordage works, boot and shoe factories, large clothing, carpet, hardware and furniture warehouses are also organized on an extensive scale.

The commerce of Montreal is well represented by the architectural character of its banking establishments, and many of the large mercantile houses. But the most substantial evidence of its importance as a commercial centre is its harbour. The solidly built basins, wharves, quays and canal locks extend for upwards of a mile and a half along the river side, and her during the season of navigation may be found vessels of every possible description from all quarters of the globe.

Two of Montreal's most influential citizens, Sir Donald Smith and Sir George Stephen, will have their names long held in remembrance for their magnificent jubilee tribute of half a million dollars, to be expended in a Victoria Memorial Hospital to be erected in Mount Royal park, Montreal. So munificent a gift speaks for itself with an eloquence which needs no other enconium.

Our Royal Family have not failed to show interest in our colonies and foreign possessions. Africa, India, Australia, have been visited by our princes ; while the Princess Louise resided

.or some time in Canada with her husband, the Marquis of Lorne, when, as Governor General, he here represented the Imperial power.

We are happy in a Sovereign who sets her people an example of goodness and uprightness, and who steadily discourages vice in all its forms.

To use Her Majesty's own words, "It has been her greatest object to do all she can for her subjects, and to uphold the honor and glory of her dear country, as well as to promote the prosperity and happiness of those over whom she has reigned so long ; and these efforts will be continued unceasingly to the last hour of her life."

If all Her Majesty's subjects can truly use such language with reference to themselves and carry it out in their conduct, we may well hope to see our country and colonies increase in strength and glory, as a benefit and blessing to the earth.

GREENE & SONS

HATS, FURS & FURNIS

MONTREAL

Beg, in this the Jubilee Ye
Most Gracious Sovereign,
their sincere thanks to t
tomers for past favors, an
retain their continued
and esteem.